Moving On

Margaret Joan Cooke

ISBN 0-9544539-5-6

Don Bosco Publications
Thornleigh House
Bolton BL1 6PQ
Tel 01204 308811
Fax 01204 306868

For Joan's dearly-loved family,
the Cross and Passion Sisters,
and all the colleagues
whose friendship meant so much to her
throughout her life.

CONTENTS

Introduction 1

Bells 2

Drifting Out 3

At the Window 4

Moving On 5

After 6

Changing 7

Destinations 8

Fretting 9

Invitation to The Ark 10

Budgie 13

Starlings 14

Whales 15

Rockfall 16

Double Take 18

Learning Curve 20

Looking At Swans 21

For M... 22

Landfall 23

Epiphany 24

Tenebrae 26

Survivor 27

Stranded 28

Walking on Water 29

New Shore 30

Applied Science 31

Day's End 32

Sleep 33

Here is Summer 34

Summer Slows 35

Blown Away 36

November Clock 37

A Child's Christmas Eve 38

A Christmas Round 39

The Setting Out 40

West 41

In Some Dry Crevice 42

Foundress 43

Fields 44

Bog Oak 45

Stone Flower 46

Angel 48

Strange Air 49

Stage Fright 50

Advice to Four Reckless Travellers to Greece 52

Presences 54

Before The Operation 55

The Mother's Voice 56

The Terrorist 58

Young Offender 60

Meeting Nelly Brennan 61

The Candle 62

No Other Light 63

Icicle 64

On being unable to imagine heaven 66

Introduction

Margaret Joan Cooke was born in Bolton in 1927. She was educated at Holy Infants School and Mount St Joseph School from where she won a scholarship to study English at St Anne's College Oxford. After graduating she was appointed as lecturer in English at Sedgeley Park Training College in Manchester. From there, she moved back to Mount St Joseph School where she worked as an inspiring English teacher until her retirement in 1986.

It was during this time when, in Joan's own words, she "lived quietly, with cat, in Eagley Bank," that the poems in this collection were written. In them she distilled the elements of her life that to her were most important: her beloved Bolton home and family, friendships, the places in Ireland and Scotland that struck Celtic resonances in her. The poems are rich in penetrating insights and underpinned by a strong faith in God.

As several had already appeared in literary magazines, Joan, after much persuasion, eventually consented to having all her poems collected and published. She died in September 2003 knowing that plans for this book were already under way. It is a fitting tribute to one so gifted that these poems can now be shared by everyone.

Bells

Laid on their backs, the bells
Gape upward. Grey mouths stir
No whispering ring of air.
Their cold tongues lie back dumb.
Dead weight, set for the drop.
But when the ringers come,
And the first hulk rolls
Over and down
On running rope,
One by one
With toppling swing
Each dead bell wakes
And upward flung
Its downsweep strikes
The laggard tongue
To clamorous tumult and all cry
We rise, we rise, we do not die.

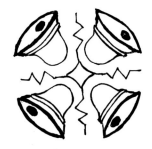

Drifting Out

She sits beside his bed in the winter dusk.
Just for a while she can do nothing more.
Doctor and priest have been. His sons will come
By a night train. She keeps the curtains open.
Homegoing footsteps pound below the window.
Car lights wash the walls. Along the street
Doors bang, children leap stairs,
The homely tea-time rituals begin
In warm kitchens. Finished with that, he lies
Still, the fresh sheet drawn smooth
Over the body's chaos, hands and feet
Quiet under the healing oils. This pause,
Strange, circles slow on dark water
Rising below. Inside the impassive head
That she can only stroke, the severing clot
Sets him adrift in time. He runs aground
Some Friday night in the nineteen-thirties,
And fingers fumbling on the quilt can't find
Shillings enough to fill the tins for rent,
Insurances and coal. He struggles, trapped,
But instantly she finds him, knows the place,
Gathers the distressed hands and pulls him clear
To drift again. Their fifty years together
Are charted in his last delirium.
Later a neighbour calls. She goes downstairs
To brew unwanted tea. Chrysanthemums
Fresh from his greenhouse tang the air. His boots,
Allotment clay still drying, stand on the mat.
Impacted time is stunned. Kettle and cups
Steady her hands, but down below the wall
By the wet stones at the water-line, the ropes
Untwist in darkness, the street sways away,
The whole house turns, slips from familiar land,
And will not find safe harbourage again.

At the Window

A pounce. Paws spatter white paint on the rug,
Whip off under a chair. He's hunting ankles.
Dangling sideways on wicked tip claws,
Spine up, ears flat, soft kitten face a clenched
Fist, defends his patch from a fur hat
On a stool. Never met bird or mouse,

But at the window, crouched behind his eye-beams,
Jaw shivering, lashes his tail at leaves
Scraping the flags. Some power within this scrap
Of fluff and wire bends him awry. His cry
Crinkles on tiny cogs. He yearns. Beyond
The glass there's life, full scope for perfect cat.

The kettle on, she's at the window too,
Waiting. Soon there'll be headlights, daughter home
From work, news, and the shopping to inspect
At the kitchen table. Evening stretches out
Predictable.

Meanwhile an inner eye
That never closes these days turns to a glass
That's dark, opaque as cataract. A pale
Thinning is all it sees, but it must look;
Feeling its powers, must yearn. Beyond the glass
There must be life, full scope for perfect being.

Street lights flick on. The year is drawing in
To All Souls' Day. The beads slip through her hands
Familiar as flour in a bowl. She prays
For the living and the dead, waiting between.

Moving On

Something is strange. Light ripples overhead
In a new place. It's late. I start awake.
And then my hand falls from the moving clock,
For you lie timeless on your high white bed.

On the last stone they'd stand, then letting go
The jetty rail, the emigrants would drop
To the dinghy's shifting floor across a gap
Of narrow water rocking dark below.

Narrow, but wide enough. For each man's hand,
Touching the harbour stones, could feel the sway
Of the full ocean bearing him away
From the loved island to an unknown land.

My strip of water rocks Atlantic wide.
Already it was yesterday you died.

After

After your thronged requiem, the priest
That sang you, bells that rang you in paradisum,
After the neighbours silent in doorways, the pub
Empty, the blown white ring of surplices,
The hush under the trees, they turn away,
Dark-suited men, women smart in black
Stepping in delicate shoes from the wet clay
To polished limousines, back to your house
Crowded with friends where, strangely, you are not.

Not in your space. Not pouring sherry,
Putting the kettle on for those who can't
Be doing with wine; not catching all the moods
Under the script, amused at honest sorrow
That heartily enjoys the good hot soup,
Or warming to the cousins absent for years;
Not storing it all up to share with her
At ease after they've gone. Not here.

Grandchildren on the stairs. She takes out food.
A leaf on her shoe. A raw hole among
The blowing wreathes. Where are you, phantom limb,
Her phantom self? When this play's over,
The funeral props dismantled, the cast gone,
The house silent, tidying done, everything
Intolerably back in its old place,
She will have time and space for such a question,
Nothing but time and space, where you are not.

Changing

If, at the land's edge, stone
Is cloud and cloud is stone,
And solid mountains ripple
With bands of shifting crystal;

If gentle shapes waver
In water, seal-smooth, soft,
Wear through waves ebbing,
Then rise up, black basalt;

If on a rock ledge lichened
And mossed, embroidered stones
Uncurl, slip to the tide
And swim, seal-thick and supple,

Substance deceives. We too,
Being more than we seem, may slip
To our ebb-tide and swim
Miraculously other.

Destinations

As if a leaf,
Knowing its gold and crimson is decay,
Should trust the wind that blows all leaves away,

And well aware
Of the leaf mould, years deep, lying below,
Look to the open sky and long to go;

As if a wave,
Among a million melting in the sea,
Should hope to keep its own identity,

And tethered fast
To earth, the tug of moon and the tide's power,
Leap to another sea, a different shore;

So are we made,
So pointed, leaves and waves that feel and know,
Beyond the fall of leaf and the sea's flow.

Fretting

Household spirit, the white cat settles,
Cream rising thick and soft around the throat.
His smile wraps round his head. His tail wraps round
His feet. He is composed. All afternoon
He'll sleep by the fire, soft and round as dough
Rising, until the child, fresh home from school,
Lifts the warm mound that loops and flops and yawns.
Her rough coat smells of winter, brings to mind
Thick-furred night, frost prickling under pads,
Glitters under grids, mouse-runs under roots,
Branchy swinging spaces, twig-ends, sky-leaps.
He struggles, won't be held, puffs like trapped smoke
Against the door, shrinks round the crack, is gone.

'Child fretting', says the ad. in 'Lost and Found',
Searching holes and ditches, listening by trees
And lock-up sheds, fretting for the lost one
That owns itself, is free, cannot be kept.
Learning grief. That may be all. No news,
Ever. Somewhere a sodden cotton rag,
Stretched by the kerb, head sunk in gutter water,
Is carted off. Or this time, it could be,
Full knowledge of mortality postponed.
After a week of waiting, the worn child,
Fixed over homework at the kitchen table,
Listening stiff-eyed to the cold sifting wind
In which no small hurt life could keep its heat,
Hears a scratch at the door, sees the lost spirit
Vault through the flap, night-wild, rain-seeded,
Rolling cold air, in each eye a moon.

Invitation to the Ark

Fur and feather, fleece and fin,
Web and wing and scaly skin,
Hoof and horn and kith and kin,
Enter in, enter in.

Lolling tongue and flaming eye
Bristle neck and cringing thigh
Pad pad padding in the dark,
Join the Ark, join the Ark.
Golden lion lying still,
Like a boulder on a hill,
Sleepy blood and glutted maw,
Chiselled mane and rocky paw,
Staring at the sun's bright rays,
Stony deserts in your gaze;
Hunting tiger on the prowl
Flickering stripes and jutting jowl
Angled eyes in diamond mask
Fanged and footed for your task
Rolling shoulders, driving back,
Roaring like the thunder crack;
Zig-zag zebra white black white
Running rings and dazzling sight;
All that leap and all that lope,
Wolf and springing antelope,
All that chase and all that flee,
Come to me, come to me.

Fur and feather, fleece and fin,
Web and wing and scaly skin,
Hoof and horn and kith and kin,
Enter in, enter in.

Enter bacillus and germ,
Enter raw and ringy worm,
Snake that flows along your bends,
A moving road that never ends,
Hopping toad and scissor frog,
All that crawl in marsh and bog,
Sliding scale and clammy skin,
Enter in, enter in.

Eagle on your craggy ledge,
Empty air beyond the edge,
Feet that grip like roots of oak,
Shoulders hunched in heavy cloak,
Pillared legs with feathers shagged,
Iron feathers barbed and jagged,
Watchful, waiting, keen of sight
As a laser beam of light,
Into space you sail and swing,
Carve slow arcs with iron wing,
Round about the sun you go
And watch a mouse a mile below.

Ghostly seagull nailed on air,
Wailing crying hanging there,
Legs stretched down and wings spread wide,
Like a spirit crucified;
Plumy osprey racing fleet
To snatch a fish in hooked feet;
All that swoop and glide and fling,
Shear the wave with level wing,
On the tossing ocean rest
And make the hollow wave your nest;
Wading birds that slowly pass
On brittle legs like jointed grass,
Plucking up your webby feet
From sucking sand and spongy peat;
Larks that from the meadow spring,
Flick the dew from beating wing
Make for the sun and soaring sing;

All that waddle, all that cluck,
Goose and gander, drake and duck,
Quack quack quack and chuck chuck chuck;
Bully magpie on the wall,
Bouncing like a stripey ball;
Creamy dove whose tender song
Grooves the air all summer long;
All that pipe and whistle shrill,
Caw and clamour, tweet and trill,
All that sing from dawn to dark,
Join the Ark, join the Ark.

Fur and feather, fleece and fin,
Web and wing and scaly skin,
Hoof and horn and kith and kin,
Enter in, enter in.

All that hide and wait for night,
Love the dark and fear the light,
All that rustle in the straw,
Nip and nibble, crunch and gnaw,
Stringy tail and skinny claw,
All that flit round barn and house,
Baggy rat and shadow mouse,
Scratch scratch scratch behind the door,
Squeak squeak squeak across the floor,
All that cower, all that quake
When owl and cat are wide awake,
All that feel around the throat
The jaws of fox, the teeth of stoat,
Snatching seed and grain and stalk
Under the talons of the hawk,
All that peep and lurk and spy,
Scamper by, scamper by.

Fur and feather, fleece and fin,
Web and wing and scaly skin,
Hoof and horn and kith and kin,
Enter in, enter in.

Budgie

Long ago your kind were caged, and blue
Australia sank in your genes like lost
Atlantis. You do not miss the sky,
Shrunk to a white ceiling, or the sun,
Caged in a window-frame, or the fresh stir
Of grasslands, dried in a little pot
For you to peck. You whistle. Whirring wings
Lob you from the bough in the china bowl
Across the wide Axminster to click seeds
At plastic chicks, wallop plastic rivals,
Shuffle on sand, busy about the husks.

A flock of voices hovers, radio quiz,
Gales off Rockall, news from the war, my voice.
You sidle dubious on my finger, claws
Little plucking rings that fit too tight,
Head cocked, eye disc trembling, ready for off,
But listening. Then your owner calls.
You grip her finger, shriek to be brought close.
Your eye pods shut to seal the mystery in.
Your head leans on the voice that's meant for you.

What do you think is going on, Geordie,
Among these beings that unwrap your sun
And make your world? You're talking to yourself,
Late night report before the cloth goes on,
Words, words, snatched from the world's air, scrambled
Messages half lost in atmospherics.
Then a voice, a scratchy telephone voice
Far off, the one that knows you, seeks you out,
Now homing in like revelation:
'Where's Geordie? Where's my bird?' Message received.

Starlings

Spotting crumbs, three are an affront,
Four a quarrel, five a rolling
Brawl, while one nips in for the loot.

Then all the gang burst from the trees,
Strut and glitter on the cut grass,
Wag about, bold, legs wide, jerk worms,

Scatter. Now they ride the high twigs,
Filing their voices sharp, alert
To join the flying factory

Down town. Thousands clock on at dusk,
Fight for a place, shove, nudge, hutch up
On classic parapets, whistle

Rivets, stun the traffic with their din.
What mess and chaos as they tack
Together their ramshackle day.

But they have mastery of space
And time. Their flung net rises, falls
On sown fields, miraculously

Meshed. From the dense roost they pulse, beat
After slow beat, till all is clear.
Of rising thousands, not one lost.

Starlings can manage. This cold spring,
Any grey membrane dawn, their chicks,
Each hatched with a beakful of tacks,

Will chip and crack right through to hard
Daylight. Now the rough round begins.
Trust them. They'll get the day's work done.

Whales

A blue day. As we leave the Sound
For the swing and sway of the open sea
The engine stops.
Murdo is shouting.
The wind frays his words.
"Whale!"
After the rush to the side
No one moves or speaks.
The Shearwater, dandled, drifts.
Somewhere in the dazzle
It will rise. It must.
Look for the fin.
All round,
Black triangles crowd, press, cut the glitter.
The bright ocean pours into my head.
Could it come up
Under the keel
And Shearwater slide
Down the sudden mountain
To a black valley below?
A scatter of shouts.
Heads turn, arms point, cameras click.
A cheer rolls round the deck.
I've missed it. It's gone.
The engine thrums again.
Over the teas and whiskies they agree:
No, not Moby Dick. A modest minke.
Fun, though.
But the whale I missed,
Unframed by eye or camera,
Unlimited,
Shoulders off the Atlantic,
Bursts the skyline,
Enters the sea of the mind.

Rockfall

Feeling the cold, you sit by a great blaze
This warm June night, the doors open for air,
And poke the fire. Or try to, but your hands,
White now but seamed coal-blue from underground,
Blunder aside, frustrated round your stick.

You were the last man down. On the night shift
You watched the pumps, read history, fed the mice,
While the abandoned workings creaked and sighed
And the black water waited. Salvage done,
Up in the cage you came, stepped lightly out,
And runabout rail card in your purse, took off
To find England. You'd looked forward to this,
Lancaster, Carlisle, Durham and York, the Wall,
Then home to unpack your tales and, winter nights,
Dance the valeta over the north-west
In old-tyme halls. It ran, the time of your life,
It flew, until the day your nimble blood
Stumbled, clogged, and the tunnel roof caved in.

Supper time. Here's your tray. Your daughters heave
You up, help you fumble in dull slippers
To the door for a breath of air. They know,
Are sure, that crouched in the coiled labyrinth,
Collapsing now from the slow seep of blood,
Somewhere behind the rockfall you're still there.

You won't be left. Telling you all the news
They search for you. They won't give up. They listen,
Wait, listen (pouring your tea, cutting
Your meat up small) to you miles under, trapped,
Tapping, tapping, faint, slow, but getting through.

No room to turn. Soon you will be forced back
From hands, feet, tongue to the last cell of all
Where no sound comes. When that last black hole floods,
Where will you go? Old miner, there was one
Buried like you, face pressed to the blank wall
Where the tunnel ended. So it was strange
That though his ears and eyes were blocked with earth,
He heard rock crack, saw in an airy space
A slanted shaft (it was not on the map)
And stone rolling away, stepped lightly out.

Double Take

Cars parked, seats claimed, the duty-free not open,
We stay on deck in the fresh autumn light
And watch, in the deep slot between the quay
And the rusty side, dark water churning wider.
We're away. As the ship slowly circles,
A girl in a red track suit, feet astride
On the last stone of the harbour wall, compels
Attention. No one else has come so far.
Arms stretched out wide, a tense diagonal cross,
Head back, turned to the ship, she does not move,
Imposing on the air some powerful will.
I wonder who she's seeing off. A young
Engineer, teacher, maybe, settling down
In his first job in London. Did he wave
At her strange stillness sliding out of sight
As the ship turns?

I lean against the rail,
Trying to live again a vanished hour.
For this is what they saw, my grandparents,
Young emigrants from Shannon, Liverpool-bound,
Their last of Ireland curving up to Howth,
And tried to hold it clear, as I do now
Going home. No farewells. No one saw them off.
Their families scattered, most to America,
And who they left behind, if anyone,
I do not know. I wonder what they felt
As the land sank and the sea ran between,
The indifferent sea, unravelling all they knew.

He'd cut no more turf under a wide sky
In lonely places. Now he'd shovel coal,
Black mountains of it, twist the gritty sacks
Across his back, that small wiry man,
And heave them onto carts in railway yards.
No more river light. Lancashire's smokey skies
And dusty furnace sunsets lit his days.
Living up two steps in a factory street,
They kept their country ways. Her house was dark
With plants crammed in the window. On the hearth
A child's pet bantam scuffled round her feet.
On summer nights he left the airless town
To bring the hay in on a moorland farm.
They never went back. Ireland floated off
Out of their reach, their children weavers, grinders,
Their children's children schooled, established, English.

A century on, though carrying different luggage,
They're leaving still. An image forms, re-forms:
Now blood loss, stanchless wound, now confluence
Of rich, turbulent streams, arterial
In countless lives.

The ship lifts, stumbles,
Hitting the edge of waves outside the harbour.
The decks clear. The duty-free is open.
The girl in the red suit is tiny now,
Enamelled ikon, catching the sun, her arms
Still wide, upheld. In blessing and farewell?
Or to draw home the exile, and deny
The separate healing that confirms all loss?

Learning Curve

Innocent of Literature, I had no
Expectations. I wanted to see the swans.
'Don't you go near them,' warned the engine-man.
'Them wings could break your legs.' There were two,
Glued to the mill lodge, solid, humped, no heads,
No legs. Whitish, wiped with an oily rag.
As my crust hit the water, one pulled up
Slowly a long neck, yellow-felted, tipped
With a small head. I threw another crust
From the paper bag held trustfully in view.
The swan turned on its disc. Close-set eyes
Black-angled down the beak, took me in.
It slid close to. The water tucked about it.
Suddenly it reared, was climbing out, webs
Gripping the cinders, neck stretched, wings split
From its sides, huge. I dropped the bag and ran
Crying back to the engine-man. My legs
Snapped all the way.

The 'visionary gleam'
Came later. I saw what Bewick saw
When his slant blade incised the steep down-stroke
Of neck and breast, the pure upcurve of back
Sweeping to white water-lily points.
The thug on the lodge slunk off. In came
Tennyson, Yeats, and the enchanted lake.

Looking At Swans

The wild swans are here, flown from the north
To winter on the marshes. In stiff cold,
Field-glasses waver. Sky and dead grass
Tumble across the lenses. Then a swan
Jerks into focus. Propped on thin legs
His bulk sways about, back-to-front neck
Rooting at a speck on a tail feather.
Such big joints! A spanner tightened them
Before black shiny plastic was wrapped round
To help him hobble on rubber webs
On the frozen mud.

No churchyard nettle shirt
A queen, tied to the stake, flung over
Wings beating about the flames could work
A magic transformation on this swan.
Never a prince. A plumber, maybe. Must
He be either? Can't I let him be
A swan? Have done making the world afresh,
Amiss, with images?

He's lurched off
Into the mere. He's changing. Dark webs fold,
Flower, fold beneath unfurling wings
That beat so passionate against the pull
Of earth you'd think he'd heave the whole mere with him.
White arcs spring. He's rising, beating back
Heaviness, thick, sluggish air. He's flying.
Marsh-hobbler, sky-struggler, earth-spirit, more-
Than-swan; this double vision won't be cured.

For M...

Since I was fourteen
Christ mattered to me.
I cannot say he intervened
but when the dancing horses of my life
spun out of control
I looked for him
standing by the engine with oily fingers.

Now I am no longer young
— and perhaps a little worn —
he hugs me
and dances
and there is lightness in his arms
and there is lightness in his way.
And when I look for him
(as now I often do)
is it sacrilege to say
Christ has a look of you?

Landfall

On Christmas Day in the morning, not three ships
But you, sea treasure, beached in our grating air.
Half-drowned in this new element, you threshed
Fish slippery, and as the thorny air
Branched in your tender lungs, your cry proclaimed
Your landfall. You are strange, strange.
That sea, that cast you out, plucks your black hair
In its retreating tide. Its grip and suck
Powers your hungry mouth. You would swallow yourself,
But your fist jerks free. Your frail fingers
Anemones, uncurl and feel the air.
The sea spins in the whorls of your small prints.
The light draws you, unwebs your dazzled eyes.
You open to it like a water flower
Translucent, quivering in invisible drifts.
You must be earthed. Your mother feeds you milk,
Wraps you in wool. You push against her palms,
Your first foothold. She holds you where you ride
Her heartbeat, charging your whispering pulse
With her strong rhythms for your land voyage.
For you are on your way. From your first hour
You are less hers, more your mysterious own.
Exacting gift, who turn to your own substance
Her spendthrift love, what is your gift to her?
All she gives you.

Epiphany

So the three kings go home, leaving
The mystery in the straw, the glow
In the shadowy stable. Sadly trailing
Hoof prints blur in wavering snow.

The homely ones are left. Warm
As stoves the looming oxen wall
The manger. Nothing here will harm
The baby asleep in the beasts' stall.

Only the gifts so gravely given,
(Kings crowding the space to kneel)
Now wrapped and in a corner hidden,
Still trouble the thoughtful girl.

Gold and frankincense declare
Him king and God though laid in straw.
But for what death is patient myrrh
Biding its time? She does not know.

A frail cry, thin as a thread,
Pulls her down to him. He's awake.
See how he quivers. Only God
Would dare become a thing so weak.

She lifts him, hearing the latch slip,
Holds him close against the chill.
Cold blows through the blue gap
At the door. The landlord brings the bill.

While Joseph bows to mystery,
Loving the baby as his own,
Down in Herod's armoury
Swords hiss on the whetting-stone.

Man made god can bear no rival.
Herod, high on pride and fear,
Speaks the word. Fresh horses sidle
Plunge and rear on the barrack square.

But God made man, accepting hurt,
Betrayal, cross and burial cave,
Falls asleep on Mary's heart
And trusts himself to human love.

Tenebrae

Camel hair cloak soft under my beard
I count the eight decades of my life
Rich as any tax collector
Fondling my turquoise beads.

I have come again as always
At this season, to make peace:
Sacrifices of the past
Are strung on the line of my life
Pegged there by prayer and practice.

Celebratory the canticles
I have sung in the temple
Counterpoint then
To the powerful clank of the money-changers.

Have I lived too long O Lord
That you never blessed me
With the love of a woman
Or the gall to make a go of it?

It was the stillness of the child
Standing unexpected in the shadow
That drew me towards him
No speech needed — recognition:

On my homeward path
His shadow soared into a star
But the woman with him
Knew pain already,

Had tasted the salt of suffering;
Her head all the while covered,
She opened the clasp of her cloak
And drew him close.

Survivor

In the spring sun warming the swaddled babies,
Easing the bonds of earth and air,
He sits in the park, old man, survivor,
Grey as the heap of grit and ice
Shrunk to a stone core under the laurels.

No one left remembers
His seas tumbling with silver shoals,
His earth gold with rasping wheat,
His bold winds riding the racing forests.
Time contracts his mortal weathers.

Stranded

Late afternoon, when high tea cleared the sands,
Under the pier was quiet, like a back street,
And out of the sun. You could work your way along it,
Jump the bright stripes from the plank street overhead,
And swing round the huge legs scabbed with salt and rust
And varicose with clusters of blue mussels
Set like rock. The smell of iron and seaweed
Stuck to your fingers.

There were things to rescue:
Lost jellyfish with indigo street map entrails,
Tiny crabs, fancy as gift-shop brooches,
That cracked and broke when you dropped them in your bucket
To take them back to sea, a long way out,
Where a quick dog flickered along the tide-line
And anglers dug for bait.

It was no good.
Everything here was dead or left behind
And waiting for the far-off whispering freshness
That swayed in restless equipoise and waited
For the moon's strong haul. Under the pier,
Nothing happened. Between tides, slack hours hung.

Walking on Water

Roll up, roll up, to the star show on the pier!
And so we did, packed in a tight, loud drum
Where people heaved with mystifying laughter,
Bright hot brass coiled from the orchestra pit,
Lights split the dark, and in a brilliant cone,
Two Ton Tessie from Tennessee
Burst like a genie from her shaking sequins
And skinned our ears with voice and ukulele
Sharp as tin.

It was strange, it was tremendous,
And when we poured out of the lighted drum,
Best of all it was night, and there we were
On a plank street out at sea, in a solid wind
That blew us inside out like clothes on a line
And emptied our heads of all sounds but itself
And the roaring tide.

Stunned, we clung together
Away from the rails where spray could pick you off
To roll among the waves that crushed and thundered
Under the planks and reared up through the gaps
To catch your feet. We were almost on their backs.

Drown or dance! Out of ourselves with joy,
We set our streaming faces to the Prom,
And dodging spray, linked arm in arm in lines,
Laughing and reeling, doing the Palais Glide,
We walked on water to the golden land.

New Shore

Sunrise. A new shore
Lifts from the tide
Smooth folded ovals
Of sea and sand
Under a blue so high
You'd think the turning wind
Had hollowed it.
Out where the sandbanks hover
On sky-mottled wings
The first child in the world
Listens to larks pulling
Their twisting threads through space,
Pokes at stout blistered seaweed,
Studies the delicate script
Of terns and oyster catchers,
Runs on the dark silk snagged
With shells, and feeling powerful
Drives the whole ocean
From a pale disc round his foot.
Idly, behind him,
The tide flicks tons of water
Light as a hand of cards.

Applied Science

Propped on an aching elbow the child stared
At the window, stared to hold the sky in place
And stop the monster furnace at its back
From blowing it right off. But trembles widened,
Bolts shook out, and as the flashing sky
Tore loose to crash on the house, her parents woke.

Just in time. She wafted the damp sheet.
His shadow, huge on the wall, turned up the wick
Of the kelly lamp. The window flickered blue.
He'd be up at five for the foundry but he stood,
Patient and mild, interpreting the sky.
"It isn't forked, it's sheet. It ripens the crops."

The child considered. Barley heads were spiked,
Fixed on tough stalks and packed with pellets.
When you plucked them from the gap in Webster's field
On Saturday walks, they scratched your legs.
If you tucked one inside your sleeve
It clawed right up your arm.

Of course. It must be true. What else could melt
Millions of stacked-up barley spears
And burn them gold to bend and roll in the wind
Up Webster's hill? So the blue furnace
That blazed and roared in the dark could take its place
In a friendly universe. The child slept.

Day's End

Day's end. The last ferry creeps
Through rising sandbanks. The thick tongue
Of tidal mud retreating licks
The channels. Past the estuary
And wet-sacking salt marsh
The sea rolls sullen scrolls
Under a slab of sky.
This is the dubious shore,
The nets of spinning sand
Where tides tunnel grassy flats
To drown unwary fowlers.
Here Amounderness,
Tangle of marsh and mere,
Seeps to the Irish Sea.
No setting sun. A cleft in cloud
Where daylight drains away.
Curlew and lark are grounded.
Glutted with mud-life
The roosts fall silent.
Nothing lifts a wing, a voice, a heart
Between these heavy levels
As the sky shuts down.

Sleep

Falling asleep
The mind smooths out
In rings riding
Deep water.
Make no sound.
Let no stone roll
From the tall rock.
Wake no dark shape,
No cleaving fin.
Keep all still.
Be found tomorrow
A bright pool
Holding the sun.

Here is Summer

It will not mend, this broken summer,
Blank as a shut door.
The lawn slides underfoot,
The mower sticks under the hedge
Where grass heaps, heavy as wet linen.
Slugs fatten under draggled leaves.
Moss huddles, tightens mouse feet
On the roof under dark trees.
Over all, the clay sky sags.

Forget expectations.
Stand at dusk by the sycamore caves
In the quiet cloak of rain.
Between the swimming boughs and soaking roots,
Where night creatures dart, shuffle and creep,
And water threads each chink and crevice,
The earth smell closes in,
Strong as the walls of a well.
Here is summer,
Powerful, now, claiming its ground,
Not to be set aside.

Summer Slows

Summer slows.
Green thickens, closes paths,
Horizons.
Netted in trees,
Gold space hums.
All time is now.

Cats in hot fur
Stretching from secret beds
Among roots
Ponder in doorways,
Look for cold sinks
And dripping taps.

In the leaf-dark kitchen,
Children dazed with sun
Tip the milk jug,
Stir slow blue spirals
In purple whimberry,
Entranced.

Flags will be warm
At midnight,
Tomorrow like today.
Time is honey-slow,
Moved only by the weight
Of its own richness.

Autumn is myth,
The crisping of the leaves the honey-crust
Of summer.
In still air,
Mounded sycamores hang
Like stone.

Blown Away

Wind in the trees
Is tossing light,
Blowing off leaves of it,
Bubbling through poplars.
Willows stream it
Through spendthrift fingers.
Sycamores thresh,
Their iron discs
Of shade broken,
Their domes dismantled,
Fan vaulting
Shrivelled to wicker.
Stripped trees rock sky
In black angles.
Roots resist,
Tighten their grip
On what they know.
Winds blow
Summer away.

November Clock

First light. A cold flowering
Of fog in bushes
White space in branches
Breath in the air
As I take in the milk.

Noon. A blown rook
Trips on rough air
Drops a feather
Black, brittle, bright
As the grain of charred wood.

Lighting-up time.
Dusk draws the street
In grey brown chalks.
The cat slips out.
Cold fills his fur.
A lingering moth
Clings to the window,
Summer wings
Etched on glass.

Night. The garden
Listens, breathes.
Two chunks of chimney
Break off, float
To the round moon harboured
In the sycamore:
Owls, thorny cries
From black hollows.

The year is dying.
In cold and dark
Frost sparks light
The white candle of winter.

A Child's Christmas Eve

It's Christmas Eve. Her head holds angels watching
The far curve of the world, a wintry road
Where early travellers toil. How many miles
To Bethlehem? They won't get here till dark.
The angels fold their wings. Out in the street
Joe Bannister the coal man shouts and humps
A sack off the cart. His horse, expectant, jingles
And stamps and whisks a crust from her palm.
She knows he wants his stable too, but it's too soon.
All day she flits about the house, restless
For riches. In the kitchen there's a goose.
Kettles of boiling water could not quell
The stubborn quills, the down drifting. Now,
Touched, cold skin slides and wrinkles. Dead. Upstairs
In the dark wardrobe a parcel rustles.
A doll? The back door clatters wide. Here's Dad,
Shedding cold air, arms full of prickleback
Holly that bounces off the floor and pale
Mistletoe berries that globe the foggy light
Of magic woods. Along the twilight path
Saint Joseph leads the donkey and Our Lady
Pulls her blue cloak about her in the cold.
How many miles? The angels rouse, keen-eyed,
Their wings ajar. As the day turns and rolls
To darkness, snow sways in the air, faints,
But will settle on icy flags, on roofs,
Out on the moors. Mother draws the curtains,
And stands her on a chair at the scrubbed table
To rub dry sage. Its hot scent fills the room.
Dad pokes the fire and wedges on the red
A split cob, sharp sides glittering black. Fresh flames
Curl under it, grip and go roaring
Spark-shot. Into air the angels rise.
It's getting late. Something begins now
To hollow her like a bell trembling to chime
If it knew how. She leaves the fire and creeps
In the dark gap between curtain and pane.
It's there. On Bannisters' chimney pot. The star.
Over the cold miles of moor they're coming.
The stable's warm and waiting, the straw spread.
Tomorrow she'll light her candle at the crib.

A Christmas Round

Christmas this year is strange.
Gathering as usual,
Children, grandchildren
Excited, present-laden,
Up the M6 they'll head
For Christmas tea, a ritual
That keeps all safe.
But there's a change.
He's leaving. Nothing said
Acknowledges that both
Are acting a brave part,
Harbouring grief.
He smiles, watching her spread
The stiff white cloth,
Polish and count each plate
For the last time.
Next year they'll hold the feast
At a son's home,
Herself an honoured guest
Sitting with idle hands.

But now all come
To the old house, crowd
With gifts around him,
Feeling too strong, too loud,
Tease, watching him smoke
The forbidden pipe, talk,
Laugh, but are dumb,
Knowing how each one sits
At a table that time strips,
At a fading hearth,
How death and birth
So strangely wreathe,
How their long childhood ends.

The Setting Out

In the close room
Holly and mistletoe
Exhale sap and leaf mould,
Air that he could breathe,
Woods where he could roam.
He drinks their freshness, cold
And earthy. He is near
His setting-out. The star
Travels ahead.

Now he must go.
They gather round the bed.
His face like snow
Thaws to dark earth.
In the still room
Nothing is
But each dragged breath.
In every pause,
Their lungs labour for him.
They listen.
The next will never come.
He is his effigy.
Tonight the star
Stands in a bleak heaven.
It is Epiphany.
Balthazar comes, bearing myrrh.

West

Hand over eyes as the road bends
Into the level sun I see
The sign at the roundabout: West.

And wherever I'm heading, West
Draws the unfocused mind. The world,
The day, roll steadily that way.

There's a sea in the sky. All round,
A tide floats land-locked hills, blue backs
Blunt heads gathering to swim west.

Men digging in gardens straighten
Their backs, turn west to watch the flood
Brimming and gleaming behind trees.

In valley towns aground in shade
A ripple on a wall, a blaze
Of estuary over roofs

And in the gaps of houses bring
People to their doors, gazing west.
There's something in the way. West is

An old ache for land's end, nothing
Between, for the clean arc of sea
And sky, the pure circle of sun

And the sun's momentum over
The rim and edge of things, not now,
But coming, when the night draws in.

In Some Dry Crevice

Feeling in the pocket of an old coat
I pull out a shell:
And a grey silk day, ebb-tide, and glimmering miles
Where a horse and rider trod sky into sand
On the last shore this side America.

I rub its back and feel
The bay's long bend,
The cream and curve of waves on rippled sand.
A sky of pearl
Rolls in its hollow where I hear
The tides of blood and salt.

All that space, that time,
Secreted in this random speck
Held in my hand, unhinged,
Its other half and proper life all gone
In long ago seas.

If ever I become an empty shell,
Out of my element and left behind
In some dry crevice, may my mind still hold
A windy shore, a sea travelling out,
A sky clearing.

Foundress

*For Elizabeth Prout
foundress of the Sisters of the Cross
and Passion*

Fire charred it.
The world's weight
Ground it to dust.
The dust cried out.
A power not itself
Gathered its trembling atoms to a point
And held it firm.
A dark world turned,
Pivoted on a point of dust,
To light.

Fields

For Sister Barbara

You worked a field
In a high place
Among folded hills,
Learning the soil,
Winds and weather,
The lie of the land,
The ways of nurture.

There were days
When fog stood
A mile high,
Your field stretched its starved pelt
Head down under rain,
And nothing grew.
What never died was hope,
Trust in the seed.
So the packed sky loosened,
The sun leapt out,
Furrows greened
And the young corn sprang.

Now your last harvest
Ripens, stands tall.
As the hills unfold,
You see on a far slope
Another field,
A stony patch,
Stones that would make
A sheltering wall,
Good earth under brambles,
Possibilities,
Work for a maker's hands.

Bog Oak

He looks at it a long time,
Days, weeks, months,
This jagged stump
Sprawled in his studio.
He thinks
How melted time drowned it,
Reeds and mosses died,
Pulled down a million suns;
How they hugged in the dark,
Snug fit of peat and oak,
While centuries turned
And the slow bog grew,
Heavy and rich with death.

Then the machines came;
In no time at all
Ripped up the smothered suns
To burn again,
Plucked from the peat's grip
This reluctant stump,
Dead five thousand years.

As he looks,
It roots in his mind,
Gives him a shape,
Stirs under his fingers.
Now he, a tick of time,
Picks up his tools.
A wild black horse,
Rearing against the bit,
Kicks from his hands
Into fresh centuries.

Stone Flower

Carving on a medieval coffin lid in Lincolnshire.

When Annette died at seventeen,
A snapped flower in the builders' rowdy camp,
Her husband, master mason, took his tools
To carve her coffin lid.
He knew his craft, the angled blows
That crack stone, split it off
To find the hidden shape.
Grief could be worked through.
He'd compose her bones,
The bright flesh fallen away,
To a new design.

The chisel's edge
Forced from the stone a difficult flower
Fit to bloom in the shut dark.
Inch by inch
It grew complete
From stemming thigh
Through calyx ribs
To budding skull,
And round the rim the clinking blade incised,
'Annette awaits the resurrection.'
So he defined her death, his hope.

Now the lid stands
Propped in the sun by the church wall,
And somewhere under the wild grass
Annette still waits.
Long ago her ordered bones
Lapsed awry in nameless dust,
Quietly surrendered
Identity.

But still the mason's flower,
Bedded in patient stone,
Bides its time,
A silent stubborn pledge:
Her flesh will cleave
To numbered bones,
Her spirit breathe
In individual dust.
Nothing is lost.
Annette will rise.

Angel

On my knees
scrubbing the cloister tiles
I dreamed of dancing
in an Eden free of serpents:
that's how he found me
sweet with sweat
ready for deliverance,
drinking in the darkness
of the shadow of his outstretched wings,
in an oasis where my body uncurled
as a rose breaks bud
at stealthy sunrise
stretching from dark to light;
seven stages of pleasure
I savoured in silent sanctuary.

Strange Air

On surfing from Classic FM to Irish Radio

No, this is not the rich vibration
Of a violin.
This air on a low whistle
Is sound stripped and clear,
Riding in
On the strong back of pipes,
A wail, a sob
In that rough music,
A long curve, a sudden swerve
To the heart,
Alien at first, then known
From long ago,
And loved.

Like a sea-bird,
Cold from Atlantic hollows,
That cries in the wind,
Circles the rock in long, slow flight,
Then flicks a wing-tip
Strikes a ledge
And settling stormy feathers
Claims a home.

Stage Fright

We don't belong here. That's the special charm
Of being abroad. It's street theatre. Sun
Hammers the square. Against a backdrop sky
Of furnace blue, the market women sit,
Solid as church bells, shouting at the crowd
With clanging metal tongues, and stowing change
In thick, black skirts. At night young men like Mithras
Challenge the bulls in the Roman amphitheatre.
Past and present. Instant. Both unreal.

Mid-afternoon in the cavernous hotel,
I'm restless, out of step. The swing door
Reflects a white ghost, a Provençal hat.
Is that really me? The street's a crack
In rock, split by the sun. In the empty square
Stones quiver under the press of heat,
Vivid and insubstantial as a stage set.
The whole town's asleep behind closed shutters.
A boy on a bike whiplashes round a corner,
Heading for home. What am I doing here?

I want rain, to stand in it, soak in it,
Throw my hat off and look up at wind
Turning the sky, shredding cloud and sun
Over my town. I want my language, tea
And talk in kitchens.

Suddenly as it came,
It's gone, that feeling of blank loss
In a foreign land. One blames the heat of course,
And the fierce light. It's easier at home,
Part of the life and knowing everyone,
To blur the question from that lucid place:
What am I doing here? Or anywhere?

Advice to Four Reckless Travellers to Greece

Study your myths with care
And beware.
For Jove descending
May provide a stickier ending
Than typhoid fever in Athens city,
Or falling in with Greek banditti.
When your traveller's cheques are sold,
Refuse all showers of gold;
One knows from history
Such loans are never interest-free.
When your car declines to go,
Never hitch a tow
From a charioteer
With a dark leer;
This
May be gloomy Dis.
If you are hi-jacked in a flowery mead,
Eat no pomegranate seed.
Such gluttonous ways
Lead to delays
Of six months or over,
Difficult to explain at Dover.
With silky bulls looking soft-eyed at you through their curls,
Where the sea unfurls,
Have nothing to do.
Vehemently eschew
All swans,
Whether friendly or not.
They're the worst of the lot.
Take flight
On sight
But don't think it's no use
If you're slower than Zeus.
Your better purpose is
Metamorphosis —
Unfortunately a change for the worse
Difficult to reverse.

Let us hope one of the four
Will regain this shore
As she was before.
She should carry at need
A plastic bag stout enough to contain two laurels
and a broken reed,
And deliver them, when the holiday ends,
To their dubious families and friends.
(Job prospects will be few,
Except at Kew.)
One final word:
Don't relax if you escape that intrusive bird.
Apollo
May follow.

Presences

Stones trembling
Round still bells;
Breath on a mirror
In an empty room.

The fingerprints
Of wind on water;
The yellow stare
Of autumn woods.

A dawn bird sawing
The thick of dark;
The split sky silent
Before the thunder.

On the edge of sense,
In the gap of heartbeats,
Strangeness,
Presences.

Before The Operation

Between wave and wave
Of a high, hanging sea,
Curved in the sliding hollow
The folded gannets nest.

Between second and second
Rocketing firework sparks
In brilliance still,
And on the darkness rest.

Between needle and knife,
Seeing familiar faces
Under the strange green caps,
The calm moment of trust.

The Mother's Voice

John's tea was spoiling in the oven
When the policeman came.
I took off my overall
And went with him to the hospital.
He drove quickly: everyone else was home
And the roads clear.
An accident on the A6, he told me.
My son had been thrown from his motor bike.
That was all he knew. We didn't talk.
At the hospital, a clatter of swing-doors.
A white-coated doctor took me
Unexpectedly past the ward doors
Into a quiet office.
I did not contradict the doctor
When he said John was dead.
John's trunk was packed
And labelled for university.
His rail ticket lay in his drawer.
He had to be in London by Monday.
These things guaranteed
He could not be dead.
Only later, when I saw
The composed, aloof body,
The cotton head,
Did I believe it.
Back in the quiet office,
Among the files of the living
For whom something could be done,
They fitted me for my new rôle:
Mother - next of kin.
They were very kind.
They gave me tea
And his camera, found slung on a bush,
Empty.

Later, I put it in his drawer
With the rail ticket
And sat empty-handed.
I could not unpack his trunk.
When the lorry's tail-board cracked his head,
Jazz, football, language, God, school, home,
Love, eighteen years'
Identity
Unreeled from the spool
And spilled in the road,
Exposed.
There is nothing left.

The Terrorist

He came from the deepest level
Of the disinherited.
The warm dark of the oppressed tribe
Bred from ancestral mould,
Narrow love, rich hate.
Nothing rooted
In that fierce ferment
But wrongs and the bitter will.
He reached for the white light
That simplified by blinding
And revealed
His gunmen heroes
Their gunmen brutes
And God his tribal god.
He was simple as a knife.

By the sprawling fires of riot
He saw their tribal masks
Swarm up the barricades,
To burn and loot.

So it seemed right
To stand in the bend of a country lane
By the side of his leader
To kill.
But as the works bus came lumbering
Along the hedges,
He saw men like his uncles puffing slow pipes,
At ease with their mates after a hard day.
Some read the sporting pages,
Some talked quietly.
They wore no tribal masks.
He could not tell them apart
As they stumbled down the steps
Under the gun.

Their shared humanity
Looked out of helpless eyes
At the blind gun,
Knowing some must die
For a label.
Which label they did not know.
The word given, his leader
Briskly sorted them:
Some, correctly labelled,
On their knees in the road,
The rest, lined up against the hedge.
These he sprayed like weeds,
With shot.

The boy sickened.
Light fractured through his tears.
His white world crimsoned
As the crying blood
Burst his constricted heart.

Young Offender

Smooth-cheeked, clean in blue anorak,
Your eyes opaque, expressionless,
You have nothing to say in court.

The stone you flung that cut an old
Bewildered head itself fell back
Unmarked, hard, cold, a tight-packed self.

Others like you, plucked from safety
By a battering tide, cast up
In the same shabby bay, can still

Awkwardly speak themselves, reach out.
What sly crooked current cornered
You, beat you back into yourself?

You and your mates, pebble people,
At every contact curve away,
Have the habits of scree, support

No one, slide from the struggling foot,
Heap on the fallen, bury him;
Disturbed, will grind one another.

Systems contain you, cannot help.
Some kind official hands lend you
A surface warmth. Released, you cool.

What will become of you, inert,
Lying around, handy, the right
Fit for any violent sling?

No one has moved you. What deep ray,
What power of love can stir your core,
Wake ingrown seed, make your stone flower?

Meeting Nelly Brennan

'There's Nelly Brennan.' Always maiden names
From school. Another old dismal woman
Had cornered us. Another tale of strokes,
Dropsy and death. We could have dodged but didn't.
I blamed my mother. She wanted to be caught.
Saturday tea-time too.
Nelly Brennan drooped,
Wrinkled, round-backed under a thick brown coat,
And blocked our way. She carried heavy bags
Of vegetables bought cheap as the market closed.
Little tortoise eyes fixed then dismissed me.
'So this'll be your youngest.' Wait for it.
'I buried Joe last August.' 'Was he dead?'
I muttered. 'He took ill in the March.'
This was bad. Five solid months to get through.
The tale meandered on, gathering facts
That clogged it. How well I knew the shape,
But not the meaning. 'He picked up in the May,
Just for a bit.' Another pointless loop.
I could tell it myself in two minutes, straight
To the requiem at St. Pat's and the boiled ham tea,
And we could all go home. The square brimmed up
With starlings and blue dusk. The town hall clock
Struck five. They'd be streaming out from football.
We'd never get a bus. 'The doctors didn't know
What to make of him. They sent him home.'
She put her bags down. People pushed round us.
And all the time, my mother, so impatient,
Quick and bright (were they really the same age?)
Stood as at a ceremony, still, attentive,
While Nelly Brennan poured on the heedless street
Her slow libation of grief. Watching them both,
I saw it. She had to tell his story,
Mark his ending. And we had to listen.
It was his due. And hers. And would be ours.

The Candle

Their smile among
Flowers, fresh sheets, stirs for the heroic sick
An awe too easy, comfortably slick.

Their long dying
Rears such a noble light we may ignore
The crooked wick crouched in the darker core.

Poor lonely wick,
White feet rising from the molten pyre,
Bears on his crumbling back that towering fire.

Himself the stake,
Plunged beyond shaking to the candle's end,
His will is fixed. He needs no other bond.

He cannot see
The holy flame haloed in spinning rays.
The tight blue fire bandages his eyes.

He cannot die.
His pain unpicks him, makes the wax betray
Fresh hidden fibres as it melts away.

No friend can come
In the strict circle where he stands alone.
It is a world with foothold just for one.

How did he come
To this white pyre? He has forgotten his name.
And was there once a meaning in his pain?

Economy
Of suffering, not understood, pure loss,
The light by which we see the dark, unless,

His last hour near,
He thrusts his burning face out of the fire,
And as he leans into the boundless air,

Another world
Opens around him that we cannot share.
He quickens, glows intense at his red core,

And headlong leaps.
But leapt with tethered feet, and the charred twist
In the stiffening wax lies spent, his vision lost.

Or did his spark,
Extinguished now under a little smoke,
Follow the flame into the welcoming dark?

No Other Light

Lord, you endured
All that we know of loneliness and pain,
Fell into darkness, died and rose again.

You know our fear
Of nothingness, the blank of senses, decay,
For you have been there first. You know the way.

No other light
Has laid across that void a shining path
To a new life the other side of death.

When senses fail,
And the poor wick lies spent, Lord Jesus come,
Be his bright track of light, his one way home.

Icicle

Out of the whirling sky,
Fragmented, lost, you flew,
Each blind flake wandering by
Feeling its faint way.
Spent, you settled.
In the glint of early light, you felt
Your random longings melt into clear purpose.
Snow drifted. Water knew
The way it had to go.

You searched for him all day,
Seeking the swiftest way but all you found
Was the level where you must keep,
Gather yourself and brim
To fullness for the leap
To the magnetic ground. And as you waited hour
By hour for your increase,
Cold hardened.
At the rim ready, you felt its power
Resisting your release.

You faltered then, your flight suspended.
As the sun, forging an iron night,
Raked to the horizon
His concentrated fire,
The cold set round you, locked
Your liquid atoms, blocked
The way to your desire.

Despairing then, you dug
The stone air, strained to drag
Your stiffening limbs, and crept
Down narrowing tunnels, trapped
At last, buried in space,
A crippled icicle.

Night thins. The light pours through.
Though your unfeeling ice
No longer knows nor cares, to him you seek
All things are possible.
As you hang helplessly,
Each ridge and cramp records
The struggles of a will set towards him.

Now you can do no more. Let be.
Wait for the thaw.
Then feel the stone air move
Your twisted crystals sleek, unlock and speed
Then flow unhindered to your love.

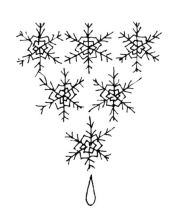

On being unable to imagine heaven

Eternal rest give to them, Lord,
and let perpetual light shine on them.

I never mean this prayer.
Beloved dead, I cannot wish you
Eternal rest, as if you could lie for ever
Lapped in a quilted box
Or stretched on marble, your incurious eyes
Lidded against perpetual light.

I would have death hold you
Like a trapped bird that beats against the window,
Tired legs awry,
Smooth your dishevelled wings
Gather your feet
And set you soaring from the open door.

When my turn comes,
After I've circled the sun,
Being earth-bound
May I slip under familiar eaves
To the warm dark, croonings,
Settling of feathers, travellers' tales.

Because he shares our nature,
Perhaps the risen Lord,
Who met his friends from the boat
And cooked them fish
On a little driftwood fire,
Will arrange this for us.